lanMcIntosh

SUCH STRANGE JOY

i.m. Mark Ogle

SUCH STRANGE JOY

Ten Years of Shore Poets

Edited by Allan Crosbie

———————

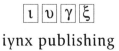

iynx publishing

Copyright © Shore Poets on behalf of the contributors 2001

First published in the United Kingdom by

iynx publishing
Countess of Moray's House
Sands Place
Aberdour
KY3 0SZ

www.iynx.com

A CIP record for this book is available from the British Library

Typeset by Edderston Book Design, Peebles

Printed by Creative Print and Design
Ebbw Vale, Wales

ISBN 0954058313

The Publisher acknowledges subsidy from
The Scottish Arts Council towards the publication of this volume

CONTENTS

FOREWORD

Now that I am exiled in London, it's easy to forget how spoiled we are by the choice of poetry events going on down here. You could go to a different venue every night for a month, (though, of course, you'd be driven nuts by the end of the second week). It is vitally important, then, to sing the praises of those organisers that provide venues and keep poetry thriving around the UK with monthly line-ups and small festivals. 'Shore Poets' has been running now for 10 years, thanks to the incomparable enthusiasm and hard work of all those involved. They have hit on a formula that works well – a mixture of music with readings from well-known names, relative newcomers and sets from the Shore Poets themselves. Most established Scottish poets have given readings for the group and with such a lack of regular reading venues in Scotland, doing a turn at 'Shore Poets' offers poets a crucial chance to display their latest wares to the Scottish poetry community. The current venue at the Canon's Gait is just right for atmosphere – slightly dark and cavernous, with drink flowing and poetry lovers newsing and carousing as folk have done for centuries in the taverns of the Royal Mile. I read lots of poems, but that is often a limited experience – you need to hear the poet deliver the words, investing them with the passion that created them. Long live Shore Poets then and I look forward to my next visit!

Roddy Lumsden, July 2001

INTRODUCTION

Why is it important for Shore Poets to celebrate their first ten years as a cultural force in Scotland? Why is a third anthology the best way to do that? And who are the intended readers of this work?

Such questions on the purpose and audience of poetry are frequently asked, not least by poets themselves, and they're notoriously difficult to answer. On the 'micro' level, starting to write a poem with a pre-planned agenda or design usually signals disaster for the artefact. Most good poems begin by chance and end, after a lot of hard labour, with the poet reasonably satisfied that they've worked out what the poem has been trying to say to them through all those drafts and redrafts. The 'purpose' is only gleaned, or guessed at, after completion. As for audience, where do you begin? Do poets write for themselves? For their lovers? Other poets? The 'reader over the shoulder'? God? All or none of the above?

Meanwhile on the 'macro' level, an anthology like this is about reminding ourselves of the wealth of talent we have to nurture, and about re-acquainting ourselves with the diverse voices which are trying to make sense of our culture, who we are and where we're going. For ten years Shore Poets have provided a small platform in art galleries and cellar bars for those voices, and pockets of space for an Edinburgh audience to hear them. Ten years seems like an appropriate time to raise that platform a little higher and to widen the space for a bigger audience . . .

And who is the audience? Well, if you have this book in your hands, it is very likely that you are one of the poets whose work appears inside, one of their friends or relatives, or a regular at the monthly Shore Poets gatherings. But all of us in that group are hoping *Such Strange Joy* will reach out beyond the Canon's Gait pub, beyond Edinburgh, beyond ourselves, because it's important for this anthology to be more than just a

10th birthday celebration, and certainly more than any kind of back-slapping self-congratulation. It's got to be a celebration also of the 'strange joy' that is reading, listening to, and sometimes trying to write poetry, and a celebration of the ways in which poetry can make us take a new look at ourselves, our country, and the world beyond it. And the more revellers there are at that party, the better.

So come in and join us – for this, my serendipitous reader, is for you . . .

A. C.
June, 2001

EDWIN MORGAN

Eggs

We gathered eggshells every spring
When I was young. It was a thing
No one explained or understood
But we knew it would not be good
If we scamped the unspoken claims.
It came round just like children's games.
Nothing but the best would do.
The slightest crack became taboo.
Speckled brown or white, no matter,
Scrape out every skin or tatter,
Wash them, lay them out to dry.
Then the moment came when I
The painter took my painting set –
I can feel the sensation yet –
With my brush curved inside each shell
To leave it blue as a bluebell.
The outsides then became a riot
Of black and orange, red and violet,
Abstract, never two alike.
We hung them from the ceiling light.
They dangled, hatching such strange joy
As could not disappoint or cloy.

BRIAN McCABE

1. Counters

Tiddliewinkled into the inkwell,
– that thimble of pale enamel
like an egg's shell, nesting
in an ancient wooden eye –

they were the counters
and we counted them: one
two, three, – but who was this
crosslegged abstraction: 4?

We added them into a column
which leaned towards infinity
before it spilled and scattered
its random pattern on the floor.

Soon they'd have us lined up
in columns: human logarithms
chanting an ugly prayer
to the god of Multiplication.

The chaos we came from
would always be there –
whatever was done
with the counters.

Those buttons of colour
we placed on our tongues,
to taste the smoothness
the thinness of 1.

from *Wild Numbers*

GAEL TURNBULL

from 'Transmutations'

HE WISHES to remember his early childhood but the more he tries, the more anything tangible eludes. Only one memory remains indelible:

of a Christmas Day, his father trying to amuse him with a conjuring trick and after several failed attempts finally succeeding, then looking to him in triumph for a rewarding smile that he was unable to give, and now never could.

ANNA CROWE

Gollop's

For Rosy

Gollop was our grandmother's butcher.
Saying his name out loud, you swallowed
a lump of gristle whole. Even the thought
of going to Gollop's made us gulp,
made my little green-eyed sister's eyes
grow rounder, greener. Swags of rabbits
dangled at the door in furry curtains;
their eyes milky, blood congealed
around with mouths like blackcurrant-jelly.
You'd to run a gauntlet of paws.

Inside, that smell of blood and sawdust
still in my nostrils. Noises. The thump
as a cleaver fell; flinchings, aftershocks
as sinews parted, bone splintered.
The wet rasp of a saw. My eyes
were level with the chopping bench.
Its yellow wood dipped in the middle
like the bed I shared with Rosy.
Sometimes a trapdoor in the floor
was folded back. Through clouds of frost
our eyes made out wooden steps, then
huge shapes shawled in ice – the cold-store.

Into which the butcher fell,
once, bloody apron and all.
When my grandparents went to see
Don Juan, and told us how it ended
– *Like Mr. Gollop!* I whispered.
Mr. Gollop only broke his leg, but
Crash! Bang! Wallop!
Went Mr. Gollop!

we chanted from our sagging bed,
giggles celebrating his downfall,
cancelling his nasty shop.
As the Co-op did a few years later
when it opened on the High Street.
Giving him the chop.

DIANA HENDRY

The Fisherwoman

So grey I thought she'd risen from the sea
to trundle her cart over the cobbles
to Market Street. Never smiled. Wasn't
one of us. Could have been an ex-
mermaid in Neptune's thrall for breaking
sea rules or loving a mortal.

She was the first artist I ever knew.
How she could behead and gut a freckled-
bellied plaice, slit a kipper to a pair
of fine gloves. Pure origami her knack
of wrapping a haddock in a sheet of old news.
I never thought she dealt in death
only in mystery and accomplishment.

I venture that at night you'd see her
sail away, her cart a gull-drawn tub,
fish jumping to welcome her like children
and she a golden Aphrodite singing.

TOM POW

Humble Pie

That concert, what struck me first,
once the waiting was done, was the size
of his head, the simian droop of his arms –
Stevie Marriot, in tight jeans and braces:
human rag-doll, heavy metal mascot.

Perhaps it was the hair; gone the neat
feathered look of *Itchycoo Park* days,
gone the tailored grey suits. Now
his hair had a botanical will of its own,
as if, like his life, it'd been hot-housed.

He'd come on with the rest, once the roadies
were through, planted his spider-boots
among the intricate web of black wires,
lifted his lips to the mike in an almost-kiss,
as the band unleashed its "wall of sound".

And he drilled, into the dark corners
of the hall, each splintered syllable,
till sweat drew his hair round his skull
and he was pale in the glare as an altar boy –
but standing his ground, giving his all.

My guess, I was probably half-pissed
or a little bit stoned, my arm at times
round her waist, head tilted, as it would be
when later, ears ringing in the silence,
I lay on the small cymbals of her breasts

watching the humdrum marvel of each star,
clear, cold and hard, burning at its core.
And with the same clarity that I recall

little Stevie's honest show, I watched
Arthur Brown, self-proclaimed *God of Fire* –

past his chart date by then, as I admit
we were too, dancing like a demon in strobes;
till some comic turned on the lights – the lot! –
to reveal a very ordinary Joe
in long johns, simply jogging on the spot.

ALISON PRINCE

Policeman

The uniform stood there with me inside.
D'you know where there's a loo? a woman asked.
My arm came up and pointed.
See the beer tent? Just beyond it, to the right.
Oh, great.
And off she went,
treading through carpets of dropped cans
and broken glass, half sandwiches,
crisps packets, bottles, Twix-wrap, foil,
thick polystyrene beakers, cardboard plates
bloodied with ketchup, scattered chips,
part-eaten pizzas, vomit, fags and mud.

The boots walked on, my feet inside,
legs in their trousers, body, head
protected. Sundry musics
came to my covered ears,
the laughter of drunk people
and non-urgent screams.
Then there was this tree,
quiet, as trees are,
standing amid the muck with dignity.
Its leaves were flickering like butterflies,
now silver and now white.
The helmet's visor let my eyes
fill with the turning leaves and scraps of sky
until I could have cried.

Then I moved on.

ANNA CROWE

Maid's Room

The combed ceiling hoards up whispers, sighs,
a crackle of anger, a creak of stays.
Stripping paper under the baking slates
you eavesdrop on the previous folk – lives
of careful garlands, furrows dull and straight –
stiff generations falling down in sheaves.

But when your scraper calls up heartbeats, dust
is suddenly tenanted, the room opening
like a kiss: the tongue-and-groove of lost
Scots pine, and in the air the sweat of resin.
And you know she is close enough to touch – skin
burnished like wood, her hair in knots; just
wakened and still in her shift, in a haze of daisies
you'll never uproot, rub out, or will away.

JIM GLEN

The Room

All day we laboured, peeling off the layers
pasted on by nameless others years before.
We counted seven in all and cursed the fools
who'd made us work; wished them hunted down
or resurrected, made to answer for the litter
of their own appalling taste.

Stripped back to dull, distempered grey
an old room reeks of its own decay
with cracks that here and there map out
an unremitting journey back into the earth.
No matter. Next day, paper and a coat of paint
was all it took. A thin yet practical veneer.

KENNETH C. STEVEN

Colonel

He comes into church with sunset cheeks,
Two sticks, and legs that deserve to be court-martialled
For their insurbordination. He brays behind me,
Tells his neighbour in a loud and whiskered voice
He cannot hear the reader or the intimations.

He is a bit of England
That has long since floated off the map; a pith helmet
And stiff upper lip that have been consigned
To the dusty shelves of history.

When he taps about the village
With his little trundle of dog and a chestnut pipe
Clamped between stern jaws, I suddenly feel sorrow
For him and all the other colonels like him,
Who do not inhabit the land they fought for

But who live on, pointlessly, in the leafy fringes
Of a high-tech world that does not give a damn
For the black and white war they won,
For the country they still believe in.

BRIAN JOHNSTONE

Empire Days

It is the end of empire and still you have not noticed.
I see you sitting silently in classrooms,
the comfort of maps and globes tricked out in pink,
a litany of possession persuaded to your lips.

Your time will bring you to an atlas of despair,
certainties mere footnotes, names in brackets
harking back to Empire Days,
to soldier's caps in creased and folded newspaper,

Union Jacks too grand for anything but flags. That rust
that grew on drawing pins has pinned you there.
I watch you as you scratch out essays,
anxious that no blot disturb the fluid of your thoughts;

watch you as the paper slubs on rotes
of capitals and dates, the import/export trade,
great men; exciting you to write long past the bell,
past change and class and attitude; past me

here, taking my position up, the windows shut,
chalk so dry it squeaks across the board,
half noticing the dust I raise in clouds,
is peppering my clothes, is whitening my skin, my hair.

MARK OGLE

Home Counties 1979

Golden stubble greens with after grass;
Blackened fields roll under the plough;
Spilled grain from the last trailers
Gathers at the kerb's edge like blown sand,
Drifts, sifts, down dry drains;
Straw streaks the scarred hedgerow.

England's autumn settles to winter;
A Union Jack flutters at half mast
Above the church tower. The Last Post
Quavers above a traffic jam
Into the hazy evening air.
Mountbatten of Burma is dead.

Mourning the fallen Empire,
Up gravelled drives,
In gardens that will soon be houses,
Never out of earshot of the cars,
Our parents relax in deck chairs,
Remembering their wars.

from *Within a Walk of The Sea*
Poems in memory of John Ogle (1915–1992)

MARGARET ELPHINSTONE

Landing

The land sways.
Far horizons help, tilting only a little.
Close things twist
And all, shift
And fall.

The smell is cedar,
The man said: hot resinous dust
Weighing down air that's damp and saltless
Only a short way in
Among the alien trees.

Home's a moon back,
(No way back),
The sea between
Endlessly, hopelessly, heaving.
The land in our minds
Covers the white bones of trees
That died before time came.
In past summers
We hacked them from the peat.

The forest breathes.

Black smoke from burning thatch
Hung in the glen till evening
Then drifted out to sea.

Cedar logs jam the bay.
Men with hooks
Leap among toppling trunks and shove them down.

The camps, the man said, are up river.

A dollar a week, he said,
If you can stand it,
To howk the forest out
And send the shaved planks home.

JENNI DAICHES

Peoria Park, Oregon

Knuckles of dead wood implode
in the dry air. A footfall is a volcano;
the brown earth smokes and the grass
cracks with heat. The river is a dark
roll of water from mountain to ocean.
Nothing can stop it. Yet something holds
a breath, stills the machines on the horizon
in the act of harvest, a shimmer on a glassy
sky, a swarm of dust, grainy
as a dog-eared photo in an old album,
or memory stalled and struggling. Something
halts the disappearance of lone
steadings pale with parched distance.
Something freezes snow on the mountains
and arrests the grey Pacific breakers
where the frontier ends. I was born
in this land and feel so at home I'm stung
by the half forgotten, and so far from home
I'm confused by the alien traverse of the sun.

ALLISON FUNK

Afterward

Amid the debris,
the wreckage of events,
it was somehow as unbroken
in its way
as the egg found in the rubble
of a levelled house
or, under the dust
that was someone's good china
once, the teacup
rimmed in gold leaf,
a baby unearthed
alive, or, most surprising perhaps,
in working order
the chimes of the quarter hour
a man heard standing atop a staircase
leading nowwhere:
amid the debris, a little melody
rung against something bigger,
louder, the megaphone of the twister,
the line she would sing to herself.

RODDY LUMSDEN

My National Stigma

One winter's night in the Princess Louise,
when a brace of shaggy moths flew up
from the depths of my tartan wallet,
the Londoners said they felt ready at last
to ask me The Scottish Questions:
inevitable ones about the kilt, the work ethic,
the repression thing, our fabled gallon bellies.
And no, it wasn't true that we were mean –
hadn't I just stood a round of halves? –
that was just the silver-shy Aberdonians
and to them, just the Kittybrewster folk,
and to the folks of Kittybrewster, just Nan
and Jim Buchan in their bungalow, tugging
a stray penny between them, inventing wire.

CHRISTINE DE LUCA

Only an Ocean Divides

Shetland 1900

I wear a strippit skirt
a hap fur when he's caald

I plait mi hair, wip hit
roond me head whin A'm wirkin

I mak ganseys an openwark
ta sell at da shop for errands

On mi back a day's kendlin o paets
kishie baand owre mi shooders

We gadder da hairst o laand an sea
Hit's a hard life but a göd een

I kerry daily daffiks o watter
twa fae da wall, twa fae da burn

A'm packit mony a barrel foo
o fat herrin ta cure fur winter

an hung oot a line o piltocks
ta dry, ta store in a tinny

A'm waited lang fur sicht o a sixern
ta come back fae da Far Haaf

Wir peerie hoose hadds
a hale family, prammed in

Da cradle is seldom empty
A'm made a boannie baand fur hit

Whin wir day's wark is dön
I lift a fiddle fae da waa

Hit pits a spring i wir step
a lichtsome lift i wir haerts

[20]

CHRISTINE DE LUCA

Only an Ocean Divides

Squamish Nation, BC, 1900

I wear a striped skirt
and a warm patterned shawl

I plait my long hair. Even though
I am old, it hangs on my shoulder

I weave hats, tunics and baskets
to trade for metal tools

On my back, a basket of driftwood
The woven band rests across my brow

We gather the bounty of land and sea
It's a hard life but a good one

Daily I carry wooden pails with water
two from the well, two from the river

I have traded barrels filled with salmon
with cranberries. They warm winter

And hung fish out to dry
on wooden racks along the river

I have watched a canoe grow small
have waited for its safe return

Our family extends across generations
That is our meaning of 'house'

I like a cradleboard upon my back
I have strung new beads for it

At special times we dance
in harmony with nature's rhythms.

The flute lifts our spirits; the drum
reminds us of our beginnings

[21]

DOUGLAS LIPTON

Wolves

for the new Scottish Parliament

The icy rain is spitting
on the pines and golden birches.
Hangings of black cloud
are torn apart by sunbursts
and then tugged shut again.

Behind us wait Przewalski's Horses,
black Aurochs, Arctic Fox, Wisent, Lynx
and the other extinct of the country.
We are approaching the enclave
of the Wolves. You hold me,
kiss me. The children are scurrying.
Our friends, too, are there
with two more scurriers
and a screamer in a papoose,
and we are followed by other little packs
of back-bitten families,
out for a day of different frictions,
weather-incited.

From a crag of varnished wood
and plate-glass
we watch those almost-
wild dogs of the north
examine their territory,
tear meat and socialise.
Their puppies play,
rollicking like boulders of fur
in a river of pure air.

There is recent talk
of re-introducing wolves

to this demi-nation
of lambs and glaikit rams
and scraggy ewes,
(and – let's face it –
hardly any shepherds left to care),
but the wolves are sure to be enclosed
or else we'd dare
to be entire again,
let forests grow,
and take our chances.

RUARAIDH MacTHÒMAIS

Pàrlamaid an Dùn Eideann?

Pàrlamaid an Dùn Eideann?
Ruigidh each mall muileann
is tòisichidh am bleith.
Tha greis mhath bho thòisich
am bùrn a' ruith,
drùdhag an siud 's an seo
eadar inc bho pheann
an Ridire Bhaltair Scott
is bruthadh thar Sruth na Maoile,
ar-a-mach MhicDhiarmaid
is tuil de bhàrdachd,
de dh'ealain 's de dhràma,
ceòl is òrain
a' toinneamh nan linntean,
's luchd-lagha 's -eachdraidh
a' ruathair ar dualchais.
Bidh feum air cùram
mu dheidhinn a' ghràin
is dè nì sinn leis:
aran-coirc is lofaichean
ann am pàipear brèagha,
ach a thuilleadh air sin
lì a' bhùrn-èirigh a' leantainn
a' cur lasair nar n-inntinnean.

DERICK THOMSON

A Parliament in Edinburgh?

A Parliament in Edinburgh?
A slow horse reaches the mill
and the grinding begins.
It is quite some time
since the water began to flow,
a trickle here and there
including ink from the pen
of Sir Walter Scott
and nudges across the Irish Sea,
MacDiarmid's rebellion
and a flood of poetry,
of art and drama,
music and song
intertwining generations,
with lawyers and historians
rummaging our heritage.
We must be careful
with the grain
and what we do with it:
oatcakes and loaves
wrapped in attractive paper,
but in addition
the sparkle of spring-water continuing
to give lustre to our minds.

ELIZABETH BURNS

On Holiday in Scotland, 1st July 1999

The day the parliament was opened
we were pottering on the beach
not thirty miles away, I and my daughters,
throwing pebbles into rockpools
gathering shells and patting the sand,
feeling the sun and wind on our skin

watching the blue seawater
that had flowed down the Forth
and was moving on now, out into the open sea,
the North Sea, off towards the coasts of Europe

and all the while the wide Scottish sky
bent over us, full of its summer light

The day the parliament was opened
was the day of the picnic, the boat trip,
the swim in the sea,
it was the day Maria came,
the day the wee one ate two icecreams,
the day of seals and puffins,
a day to write about on postcards,
a day to remember all your life

the day the parliament was opened
and was found to contain
song and poetry
– things that you want from a land

Later, when we had gone back across the border,
it was enough just to touch the petals
of a white rose after rainfall

that was enough
to crack the heart
like a mussel shell
crunched underfoot
on hardened sand

STUART A. PATERSON

Home Truths

Onon from Mongolia shines wet
happy eyes in my direction as she tells
of eating roasted marmot in the hills,
grandmothers unlooping and cooking
guts and eyes and brains with savage skill.

Yasmine laughs with memories of when
she chased elephants from the rubbish bins
as Zambian mornings bloomed to ruby
over a lake the size of Ireland.

Joseph's wide eyes put into words his days
of reckoning in a Navajo sweat tent,
becoming like the snake and going down
deep to meet his forbears in the desert.

Rachel from France remembers how, when poor,
she trapped the sparrows on her window sill
with broken glass and elastic bands,
four at a time to make a decent potful.

How, then, to add my own small footnote . . .
that I met a man who said he'd seen strange
undulations by the east shore of a loch,
got all five stations through
an old coat hanger at his island croft,
who slept a week then woke to find himself
clean-shaven, who drove two hundred miles
and ended up outside the bar he'd left
three hours before and swore that once, just once,
he watched the Brodick ferry leave Ardossan,
on a calm sea, at the designated time?

Such quandaries and questions cannot rank
with how to steer Egyptian dhows the length
of Africa or Himalayan treks.
Nor should they. These are quiet folk who'll sit on
stools by darkening gantries, with no more drink,
no introduction, before they'll turn to
earn another with the soberest of winks.

St Orage

Preserve us, St Orage, Patron Saint of Warehousemen,
you whose image stares down on our weed-snagged
railway sidings and choked factory yards; whose relics
crumble in a cardboard box in a hampered lock-up
somewhere. We await your word.

St Eadfast and St Alwart, we rely on you
To indicate the Good Path, however stony.
Lead us not into that rock-strewn gully
clogged with St Randed's bones.

Oh Lord, we know your faithful
knew more deaths than we had fingers –
St Ifle and St Rangle and St Arving and St Ab, all
flew into your mercy through their disparate anguishes.

But most of all, remember us yourselves,
forgotten saints we here commemorate:
St Agger of the drunken brawling praise;
St Ainless, martyred on the lopped branch of his perfect life;
St Anza, stunned by her own reverberating song;
and blameless, maculate St Igmata, dead and forgiving child,
who even in the crib, they say, held up her little punctured hands
in wonder and in ignorance, and cried.

DILYS ROSE

Answerers

called when
we were   the cold cry
when   of the hereafter
                              snaked across

the desert of

eternal night

hypnotic

insistent

we could do

nothing to resist

the summons

to pick up our tools

wipe the tomb dust

from our eyes

with no hope
of respite from
perpetual labour
we confronted
our task:

an infinity
of starlessness
to be tilled.

[Ushabtis or Shawabtis (Answerers), mummiform figurines, accompanied the dead to the afterlife to perform agricultural tasks on behalf of the deceased. Up to 400 could be found in a single tomb, suggesting that the afterlife of ancient Egyptians was not imagined as a place of rest.]

RON BUTLIN

Him Upstairs

No more than a moment past I met him, stumbling
his way down. A bad night by the look of things:
he hadn't slept, or else he hadn't woken
and the dreams – as well they might – had just kept coming.

Should I have stopped to say hello? Caught his eye?
Polite but firm, should I have grabbed him? Told him
to get himself back up those stairs to where
he'd come from?

He pretended he hadn't even seen me.
A little late for that, I thought.
We were almost level when . . .

He tripped, lost his balance, sprawled forwards –

Was he trusting that I'd catch him? That invisible angels
with invisible wings would bear him off to safety?
He showed his celebrated mastery of circumstance:
his arms stretched wide ready to swallow-dive,
ready to take up crucifixion-mode.

And so we passed. Him falling and/or flying into another miracle,
me without a backward glance.

*

Upstairs I've found a crumpled sky upon the floor.
Torn, kicked and trampled on; holes where stars have been ripped out;
midwinter darkness clawed to shreds leaving
constellations scored across the night;
the blue of a summer's day spattered blood-red.

Such stillness. No sense of loss, no consolation. Merely nothing.

If I stand here long enough will I remember
what happens next? Already,
it seems, I have been here forever.

PAULA JENNINGS

Three in One

In a shawl of surf
there is a baby,
complex as a shell.
She has already seen
too much, the moon
has rained down on her,
blistering her silky head
with the secrets of tides,
and stars have twinkled
ruthlessly.

       A woman
strides the winter beach,
the air is wide enough
for her to breathe now,
she draws it in, drinks gold
from a rim of sky
and, reaching out,
lifts the horizon.
A girl steps through,
shy in her new breasts.

There is so much to tell.
Woman and girl laugh
together, heads bent close,
wade into the surf
to find the wise baby.

KEVIN MacNEIL

Call

night's loneliness
deepening in that anonymous
bird's meek and three-note call

The Old

the old bodach
at the leafy grave; how his
walking stick trembles

(*bodach* = old man)

The Sun's

the sun's
penetrating glare lengthens
the scarecrow's shadow

RICHARD PRICE

All Light

All light is bundled
blind into extremity's definition, the black hole –
calibrated by darkness, by
density's ideal.

Energy, as well, can't resist –
forgets its private struggle,
gathers presence before oblivion, in a high style.

How can what be known?

It's all one to me, all of us, and the past –
jealous of the helpless,
kissed and crushed,
laid summarily to rest – that's the future, with no fuss.

"More mutters on dark matter."

No-one sees inconsequence like a stargazer,
or knows nothing so well.
"Park that radio-dish somewhere else, can't you?"

Questions, questions, questions.

Remind me what planet I've earned, what year this was going to be?
Security, get lost. You're tomorrow's ifs and buts
tallied against community. You're
untold loss with a cartoon sigh and a mope –
velocities of near-love.

When? When? When?

Xerox me Gravity Simplified when you've solved that one. No –
you can send instead your A–Z of the unknown universe.

Zero-worship – nothing's better.

ROBERT CRAWFORD

A Moment of Your Time
for Kate Whiteford

Z-rods and a Pictish hoopla of carved rings
Swim into view. Yachtsails on the North Sea
Tack back and forth, xeroxing other summers
When other yachtsails did that too, sped, idled,
Veered into light. Dwamtime. Heat-haze. Relaxed,
Unchronological ribbed fields. Leylines
Flounce across territories never ours,
Where we belong. Grassed-over souterrains
Rich with mud-rhythms, moss-haired residues
Of moon and beaver, lily, loon and quine,
I praise you all. Wind-sough, wind-sook
Of chamber-music, cairn-singing, firths'
Haar threaded through a net, babbling with dew,
Murmur me, let me catch another's breath,
Lightly, as part of breathing. Here it is:
Remnant, keepsake, rune, God-given script
Made just for you, the right lines, sacred text
Of matter cooked in stars, instantly endless
Then passing on but holding nothing back,
Good for the child, the skeletal, the green
Foliage-bank whose sap's stared into at
Eye level. Here's the whole shebang that is
Time, place and climate, ebbing, dancing, set
In stone and motion, calmly at the ready
Before and after, purled in helices,
Every last atom pregnant with an A.

ANDREW GREIG

Orkney / This Life

for Catherine & Jamie

It is big sky and its changes,
the sea all round and the waters within.
It is the way sea and sky
work off each other constantly,
like people meeting in Alfred Street,
each face coming away with a hint
of the other's face pressed in it.
It is the way a week-long gale
ends and folk emerge to hear
a single bird cry way high up.

It is the way you lean to me
and the way I lean to you, as if
we were each other's prevailing wind.
The way we connect along our shores,
the way we are tidal islands,
I'd settle for that. The way
you rise up by degrees, the way
I pick sand off myself in the shower.
The way I am an inland loch to you
where a clatter of white whoops and rises.

It is the way Scotland looks to the South,
the way we enter each other's houses
to leave what we came with, or flick
the kettle's switch and wait.
This is where I want to live,
close to where the heart gives out,
ruined, perfected, an empty arch against the sky
where birds fly through instead of prayers
while in Hoy Sound the ferry's engines thrum
this life this life this life.

JOHN BURNSIDE

Shore Life

These are the creatures we love
and take for granted;

split from their shells
or sprawled across drying sand,

they yield the colours
we have yet to name

with any certainty:
that pink you see in ashes, or the fade

to petrol blue
you sometimes find in rain.

Deer in the hills,
or hares, or the questing owl

are gathered in another mystery;
larks in the field

are too involved with light;
but something of the stranded razorfish

is what we best remember of ourselves
when we are lost, so far from flesh and salt

we might be phantoms
locked into the chill

of fictive loves,
or someone else's gold.

JIM GLEN

Sunday Harbour

Fishing boats keeled over in the mud
and the tide's spewed up the usual stuff:
old rope and tyres, roofing felt,
tin cans and condoms.

Two gulls contest a meal
(remains of a pudding supper)
above the rattle of tambourines
from the gospel hall
as a wheezy organ puffs away
to a hymn that's filled with anchors
in the storms of life, or empty fields,
the harvest safely gathered in.

Out here the gulls keep being gulls,
contend the one remaining chip.
Unmoved, the sea lies stiff and grey
as concrete all the way to Fife.

VALERIE THORNTON

Partick Beach

When the Clyde Sea
turns its tide
these sandstone castles in the air
will melt to dunes.

At the high water line
nuggets of tumbled glass
and driftwood with sashcord tails
wait for a Partick beachcomber.

Those flaking slates
reclaimed from descaled roofs
will skim a dream
on the ebb tide

and, as the light cools,
the moon will pull
frothy curtains
across the mouths of shells.

ALAN JAMIESON

Speaking to the Ocean, Glasgow

What are you to me, red city of the western sun,
but a warm womb? Your European chic,
your transatlantic cheek so deep ingrained.

Warmth – even from that wee otter-man
the other night – pished an pissed himsel –
the stink of puke around him, who
on the late-night Queen Street platform
brought me the spark of light I needed
in return for a speed rolled fag,
(his hands were shivering).

Is it that your stone retains the evening's warmth –
enough to see the hapless, somehow, through?
No, people die here too, hungry and empty,
unborn potential scattered through your rainy streets
unravelling, like a broken string
that might have led them to the surface, now
a pointlessness that sweeps around the labrynth
of alleyways and all the crumpled papers.

Something garrulous about you makes me wander anyway,
draws me to the river and its empty banks,
as if your energies still drift towards that setting sun –
braving the channels with a big braw heart,
then a full sail set for liberty,
(an wi a wee bit luck, a fortune too).

'Born again at forty', I drew my last 'first breath' in you,
your air hanging like the reek over Babylon,
blessed by the presence of running water.

Painting Fish

for Sophie

The markings on her thornback ray
Are perfect, as if each one bore the imprint
Of God's little finger as, it is said,

The haddock's do, of Peter's thumb.
Her crab is bright red; her lobster brilliant
Blue. Her nurse-hound is a blur, apart

From its eyes and its teeth. Her conger
Eel is luminous, blue-green, with a grin that
Could kill. Her tour-de-force, however,

Is her pair of yellow seahorses, tails
Entwined. She has managed to capture their
Fluttering fins, their gentle swaying,

To and fro. The female's bowed head
Mirrors hers, as she sits, bent over more
Sheets of paper, eager for the others

That are yet to come; her blood-orange
Starfish; her half-hidden hermit; her gap-
Toothed catfish, the colour of stone.

NANCY SOMERVILLE

Dead Gull, Loch Brandy

On the boulder strewn lochside
your body lies twisted.
Beak open in a silent cry,
wings catching the wind
as if attempting
one last flight.

The cause of death is a mystery
to me
but nature's investigators
carry out their own post mortem,
leaving your rib cage open
to the scrutiny of the sky,

your black beetle eye
glances my way
then crawls from the socket
revealing a skull teeming
with tiny lives.

Your feathered shroud
retains a soft and vital sheen,
its whiteness matching
the summer's persistent pockets of snow.

I rise to take my leave
and about my ears the rest of your colony
conduct a raucous consultation
on the level of my threat
to the coming generation,
now curled snug inside their shells.

The loch nestles in the corrie,
preparing for the demands
their arrival will bring.

MARK OGLE

Old Farm Machinery

Rusts back to the colour of the earth
It was designed to tend.
Long past a hope of salvage or scrap
We let it lie abandoned at the corners of fields,
In the waste land behind the dairy,
To a slower death even than the trees.

Outliving our ends,
Skeletons of frail metal,
Glimpsed through clumps of tall nettles,
Your flesh flakes off, red in my hand.

GILLIAN FERGUSON

Tiger Moths For Drawing

Moths for drawing. Coloured wings blurred white
and brown like a burnt love letter; fire still frilling tips,
just furring red helmeted heads, tiny Viking horns.

Clawless tiger moths pawed to death, a cat's padded
claps as the door's night light – witch-warning as a
blood-berried rowan – beaconed biblical swarms,

maybe breeding. A large jar gathered of gorgeous
corpses, a shuddery glass mass grave. On pencilled
paper they still look alive, full of blind moon flights,

mothy sky thoughts – dead immortals. And creepingly,
in my eye's round corner where ghosts cross, bats flicker,
shoplifters lift, a stirring. Look, a Holocaust horror of

multiple limbs, and wings, moving – the dead, the half
dead, and the coming to. Only stunned. I shake them on
the window sill with a sound like crisps, kill the fascinating

lamp. As if drugged, drunk on death, the living whirr
off chuggily like injured planes, reluctantly, to tickle
the swallowing black night throat. Leaving their colour-

thin ghosts flying in white paper air on my desk. As if
the dead stay unchanged, drawn in the black-edged pages
of memory. Lie down still, well behaved as their skeletons.

STEWART CONN

"Koi Carp... Kyoto"
by Elizabeth Blackadder

Glazed but lit aslant, so reflecting less
than a pool's surface, her Koi carp
enter our world from mysterious depths.

Left of centre the largest, blotched
orange and white, seems caught
in mid-plunge. Others flick their tails,

veer and pout, flaunt their colours,
gaudy geishas for whom existence
means eating, then being eaten.

Dusk falling, light-slivers quiver
on velvety fronds, ribbons of jonquil
thicken to gold, cobalt to fathomless blue.

Part of me, going with the flow, thinks
back to those days when the fear
was of falling into the latticed pond.

Another, conscious of fiercer currents
resists looking round, lest a dark shape
should come looming, jaws ready to snap.

IAIN CRICHTON SMITH

New Year

The Old Year turns its rusty hinge
and the New Year steps out bright as a child

onto the floor of blue linoleum.
The redbreast is pecking at the bread

and the nuts lying on the frosty plate.
The child looks at it, then at the bullying crow

and learns its first lesson.
                              However,
it hears two doves cooing in the wood

and an uncontrollable joy seizes it
so that it dances barefoot on the floor
blue as the sky and quite reliable.

Later that night it sees intricate jewellery
winking at it companionably from space.

IAN McDONOUGH

Dawn Train

Through parted clouds
The world's wound gapes,
Viscera
Streaked across the sky.

Even the old among us
Wince and gasp,
As morning's insurrection
Demands we heave and strain,
Bodies briefly
Too large for our frames.

Like a ripped tent,
Night admits
A stream of photons.
Blood stirs and agitates,
Then boils
In the arterial scarlet of another day.

FRANK KUPPNER

Renfrew Street

More than once I have gone down this pleasant street,
this pleasant, slightly out-of-the-way street on the route
back from the station to the ground-floor room where I live
because of the memory of that Pakistani woman
who, in an absurd high box of a building, leant out
from an upper window in a wonderful early evening sunlight,
God knows why, as if looking for something legendary,
but perhaps only the arrival of an expected car.
She stood there in total silence. However, since I
was admiring a bright clutch of sunlit spires on the skyline,
my eye was caught by unexplainable colours nearby,
and I looked across and saw her, leaning as if to provide
a whole newly cleaned tenement building with an apt figurehead
before it sailed off enraptured into the pure, drenched, limitless light.

KEN COCKBURN

Housesitting

A bigger place, semi-detached,
nice garden, only a couple of months
and not that much further for the school,
why not? An adventure. Their offer accepted.

Contained, considered, no excess, a kind
of poem, our small flat here – replaced
by spacious there, a kind of novel,
rambling, inventive, unfinished, each chapter
sketched, but not definitive –
those early days we were forever
up and down the echoey stairs
for things misplaced (like elusive quotes),
our stuff scattered, and muddled with theirs;
the strange paintings and the strange cats,
the strange haphazard spaciousness
with a capacity for argument
far greater than we had at home –
not, I took it, a space for poetry.

It needed the animation of guests:
there was Alice's party, *now you are 6*;
Corinne, stetched out on the sofa
and Martin rippling the broadsheets out
around himself; the dinner party
we rearranged the yellow kitchen for –

but the garden (the outdoors episode)
never really happened, a cold spring,
though the children belted around in coats;
otherwise short stays on the bench
beneath the elm, still skeletal,
warmed by tea or anger sometimes –

returned, they uncorked their bottled south
and while I'm happy to be written out
to attempt the revision of our own measure,
to perfect the space we grow within,
I still, in passing, look out for the elm
now thick with leaves, the words of a tale
it's forever rattling off to the wind.

ANDREW GREIG

An Investigation

What has passed here
to crash the computer,
wipe so clean the answering tape?
This chair aligned precisely to its desk,
a spotless microwave, a well-stocked fridge,
the empty pack of condoms by the bath ...

Lower your eyes, those slooshing cans.
You are standing in the epicentre
of a non-event so absolute
there's no one left to question:
no victim, witness, not even a child
hiding in a room upstairs.

Perhaps that is the crime,
for something in the unscribbled walls
and the underlying order, as it were, implies
though women have passed through
(photos of weddings and first babies)
there never have been children here.

It's peaceful, certainly. It could be
the life of a gay man, yet some sinking
feeling tells you it is not.
Take a seat, make coffee, eat the last
slightly stale rock bun
as you make your notes and reach
the only possible conclusion.

Open the windows, pour
the petrol of this yearning.
Throw down your glowing cigarette and go.

IAN McDONOUGH

Back

Rainwater and memory
pool in the hollows,
sew a silky skin
over pocked and littered lanes,
irradiate
the dark and shuttered suburbs
of sidereal time.

Inside, a swelling tide of talk
rushes the photo-studded walls,
washes into attics,
refreshing dessicated hurts and treasures.
Neurons, long asleep, fire up
like old toy racing cars,
batteries
surging with fresh volts.

Wading out into the coddling night,
I try to shake the voice
of my integral guide
blethering weathered histories
inside my saturated head.

This village is the sea that spawned you.
This house is the boat that launched you.
This body is the lighthouse
that you sail around, and to, and from.

RODDY LUMSDEN

Quibble

Most things are possible: you cannot grasp fire
but a well worn hand will hold a stone
hot enough to scorch whatever needs scorched.

Some glazed-over madman, in a bottom drawer,
has the stratagem for time travel
or a tincture to make you seventeen forever.

Nothing is missing, is merely mislaid:
a jackstraw rickle of bones at the foot of a cliff,
the wedding ring fifty feet deep in a landfill site.

El Dorado and the hippogriff, ectoplasm
and the square root of minus one
are all there in my book, although the experts

must be on to something since they tell us
there is no word in Spanish for silence
and no known word in English for   .

ANNE MacLEOD

Harpsong

there will be nights when music is the line
we breathe, the air we curve, the innocence
bereft of logic, learning compound time

or that's the rumour. And okay, it's fine
to linger on the strings, to dampen, pluck
but there are nights when music is the line

and nights of other narrative; the primed
repeating dancing phrase requires a hand
now deft, now magic. Cleaving compound time

is not inevitable, words define
the chord (though there are times
when music is the core, the spine.)

To breathe is not a simple act, to sing
still more confused. Beyond the open throat
and warp of logic, lilting complex rhyme

proves inaccessible, air faltering
depleted. Insecure though gut-strings swing
bereft in plastic or diffusing time
still there are nights when music is the line

BASIL DU TOIT

Sound Engineer

Ums and ers, blurts and stutterings
fall to the studio's cutting floor:
a word surgeon is at work, healing
my blemished, badly spoken sentences,
removing gristly mishaps in my delivery.

She scans the tape, running it backwards
and forwards to identify ugly glottal lumps
in the vocal tissue; finds one, snips it out
and neatly closes the gap: a noisy swallow
lies on the floor on one inch of tape.

I listen in amazement as she isolates
a sigh – removes and transfers it intact,
this tiny puff, into a different utterance:
my phrases breathe more freely now,
flowing through uncongested channels.

Her art focuses on Saussurian particles,
swapping morphemes and phonemes around
like someone transplanting a cornea.
She's a language beautician, performing
nose jobs and tracheotomies on speech.

I end up speaking like an angel, in a purified
dialect of correct and necessary sounds,
while around her feet, on snippets of tape,
inarticulate phonic fragments of my voice
continue to gulp and hiss and croak.

KENNETH C. STEVEN

Geese

This evening
I went out with a basket of clothes
To hang dry in the wind. Above the wood
I saw a silver brooch of moon
Molten among the trees in the fierce blue nightfall.

I heard them first. A hundred thousand
Ragged voices clamouring against the wind
And I stopped what I was doing
To look up, to listen, knowing somehow that this was bigger.

I saw them, a rippling of backs, of wings,
That caught the moon and made waves of its light
Like the quicksilver of the Atlantic's ripples
On a white shell beach.

I listened to them until the sky took them
And even then I listened, a towel hanging from my hand.
All night I have listened to the memory of their passing, lost,
As the clothes billow like ghosts in the moonlight, wind-blown.

MARK OGLE

Wild Geese Feeding

Wild geese at sunset follow their earthbound shadows,
Seeming like sheep or cattle to graze
Stooped over their unvarying food forever,
Yet able instantaneously all to rise
From the green table when the mood
Springs them from chains of appetite,
And they complete a painting of the sky,
Slipping low and fast in a ragged arrow
Honking through cold currents of air,
Over barely touched lands and seas
Knowing when and where and how to fly
Unerringly beyond the island's canvas,
Beyond the contrivance of the compass,
Necks stretched straight for the magnetic Pole.

JIM C. WILSON

The Crossing

I drove you across Scotland – and then back again.
We sat and watched the road in front, the quiet
Ayrshire hills, and miles of unfamiliar fields.
You said the roundabouts confused you;
I missed some signs yet we never got lost:
we just crossed Scotland, side by side. You talked
and laughed while, all the time, I gripped the wheel,
forever steering – eyes on the broken white line.

I drove you across Scotland – and then back again.
That night, my wife, your family, waited;
and what was there for me to do but embrace
a friendship, unique and new, as, over
Livingston, the clouds grew thin, revealed
a way to go, beneath a clear March moon?

BRIAN JOHNSTONE

In Passing

I wander, aimless through the house, to discover
you have left, on a table in the porch,
a plate of strawberries rescued from the rain;

the first downpour of August saying:
summer passes, fruits will rot
if not collected in the gaps between the showers;

and lying there, eight blood red hearts
still warm aginst the white cold of the plate,
they hold the pulse of seasons willingly;

willing me to take their musty sadness,
press it to my lips, tongue sweetness, tang and texture
as I pass them round the cold white of my teeth,

suck every tone and fibre of the balmy days,
lay it up against recurring downpours,
against the way we have of laying fruit upon a plate.

DON PATERSON

A Meal

You know the old woman who swallowed a fly?
I mean, like – how that flutter in the ribcage
becomes a vagrant itch, this gnawing … maybe
when we die, they'll find the nested skeletons
of all the lovers that we took to eat the last …

Aye, maybe not – more likely – what's that line –
"the black egg of his unhatched disappointment".
Y'know, I still think that a man could get through life
without feeling a single thing, so long
as he had a taste for some *grotesquerie*.

Here – this'll put you off your dinner –
some Himalayan climbers recommend
an English tapeworm in a glass of milk
before the flight out as the best deterrent
to the rough advances of its native cousins.

That's how I think of marriage – one brave gulp,
a stifled gag, then give it a few months
and you both lie threaded through each other's guts
like those flourished loops on *Rex* or on *Regina,*
a royal seal set on the heart and loins …

Sorry. Are *you* hungry? It's funny,
but just then, when they met above the menus,
our eyes were bigger than our stomachs … right,
let's force ourselves, before the pain comes back –
I'll tell the waiters. *Now. Bring on the horse.*

NANCY SOMERVILLE

Risotto Marinara

Sitting in the Europa,
grabbing a bite to eat
before I meet up with the girls,
I'm leafing through
the book I've bought,
a story-board screenplay.
Picture the scene:
    American road movie
    big desert
    red convertible
    trunk full of narcotics
cynical voice-over in my head,

then a doorful of cool night air hits me
and I look up
adjusting my perceptions ...
The traffic flashing past
is keeping left,
the voices saying their good-byes are Scots,
as others calling out for drinks,
the waitress is bringing my order

and the fact that it's the same dish we had
that first night
is more to do with my taste buds
and poetic licence
than any deep and meaningful desire
to be close to you through food,
isn't it? And anyway

I'm not thinking
about you at all.

KEN COCKBURN

Singles Night in the Palace of Surfaces

He checked his five o'clock shadow in the glass.
He checked his cupboard, and made a list:
red wine, olives, chocolate (plain),
sugar, light brown, 500g,
coffee, 1 pack, Mountain Blend.

River Deep Mountain High was filtered in,
and the light overhead deleted shadow
(making Peter Pans of the lot of them).
With *Heart of Glass* the first eye-contact came –
was broken, her messages were much too plain.

TRACEY HERD

A Letter from Anna

I tiptoe the distance from the bedroom door
Across the thickly carpeted, cream-coloured floor.
I might be crossing a country or a mountain stream
But I have travelled further for much less,
And for you I would travel on foot
Through the pine forests covered by snow and ice.

Although practical in every other sense,
I have lost my heart to you, my love, and I,
Even with my dark dreams of death
Have thoughts like small night-fires
To warm my freezing fingers by, now unadorned
By the thin gold band and the vows I made
To my husband to be faithful and a good wife.

I no longer dance gracefully at parties, flirting
Thoughtlessly in my small-waisted flaring dresses
And make small talk with the select list of guests.
I am no longer welcome at their grand palaces
And my gems lie dully in their velvet-lined box:
The emeralds are flowers shrouded by winter
And my diamonds are grey in a storm-burdened sky.
Only the rubies are bright and that is an ill-omen:
My blood runs cold in these brilliant stones.
Now, I will tell you our story as I wish it had happened.

Your beautiful mare would never have fallen, she'd
Have finished the steeplechase at the head
Of a procession, every bone in her body unbroken
And now, she'd be grazing the paddock with her colt
By her side. For me, there would be no walk
To the station, no pause in the shadows away
From the lanterns and no departure, with the great

Black train's wheels in slow motion as I fell forward
Into the oil-stained tracks. We'd be lying here,
Under white covers, two children lost in the benevolent
Forest, clutching each other to stave off the cold
And patiently waiting for a Russian spring.

PAULA JENNINGS

In the Late Night Gallery

After Sotto Voce *by Maxine Greer*

At first I see just painted strings,
a thicket from ceiling to floor,
with denser darkness at its centre,

simply twine and spotlit gloss,
but with a shift of weight, sleight of eye,
the space between the strings becomes

thin windows, strips of ice, or crystal pipes
from some fantastic organ. Breezes whine
and chime through brittle tubes

and coalescent air invents rooms,
a castle of glass, perhaps a princess
locked in rosy stasis, waiting

for her poisons to be lanced
upon the lips of some hero,
who is really her own self, stronger,

waiting in the late night gallery
where strings are brambles
and the artist transforms air.

JAMES McGONIGAL

Turning Over in a Strange Bed

Living with women is like turning
over in a strange bed at night
and trying to find your watch
and trying to read its face

or like living in a landscape
which is Donegal to your Galloway
with something like the same hills
with nothing like the same water

splashing down to a greener sedge.
Alongside your road they run like a river
your road follows valleys carved out by water
that is still peaty enough and cool

to quench your daily thirst.
Their blood is legendary and their sweat
on the right occasion never to be forgotten
while their tears remain unpredictable

by any instrument you will ever possess.

JAMES McGONIGAL

Ag Casadh Thart i Leaba Choimhthíoch

Is ionann a bheith i do chónaí le bean
agus a bheith ag casadh thart i leaba choimhthíoch san oíche
agus a bheith ag iarraidh d'uaireadóir a aimsiú
agus a bheith ag iarraidh a éadan a léamh

nó a bheith i do chónaí
mar a bhfuil dreach na tíre cosúil le Tír Chonaill seo agat
i gcoinne Ghallobhagh seo agam féin
le mórán na cnoic chéanna
ach gan a dhath den uisce céanna

ag stealladh anuas go cíob is glaise.
Le gruaimhín do bhóthair féin
ritheann siad mar a bheadh abhainn ann
bíonn do bhóthar ag reáchtáil gleannta a snaidheadh leis an uisce
atá fós móintiúil go leor agus fionnuar

le do thart laethúil a mhúchadh.
Tá cliú agus cáil ar a gcuid fola
agus a gcuid allais ag an tráth ceart ní déantar dearmad air go brách
agus a gcuid deor ní féidir a réamhinsint

le gléas de chineál ar bith a bheas agat ariamh.

trans. Rody Gorman

[71]

ANNA FRATER

Semaphore

An e na brataich cheàrr a tha mi 'cur a-mach
's nach tuig thu an teachdaireachd
a tha 'gluasad anns a' ghaoth?
An e am pàtaran a tha ceàrr
neo na dathan
's gu bheil thusa 'leughadh rud nach eil mi 'g ràdh?
Neo a bheil thu ri cleas Nelson:
a' toirt a chreids nach fhaic thu
gus nach bi agad
ri freagairt a thoirt dhomh?

Fiamh

Fiamh a' ghàir air mo bhilean,
fiamh an toileachais 'na mo shùilean,
fiamh an t-sonais 'na mo chòmhradh
fiamh an eagail 'na mo chridhe
's mi 'tuiteam sìos dhan dorchadas.

ANNE FRATER

Semaphore

Is it because I'm hanging out the wrong flags
that you can't read the message
that's moving in the wind?
Are the patterns wrong
or the colours
making you read it all wrong?
Or are you, like Nelson,
pretending you can't see
so you don't have to give me
an answer?

Tinges

Tinge of a smile on my lips
tinge of happiness in my eyes
tinge of contentment in my speech
tinge of fear in my heart
as I fall down in the darkness.

GAEL TURNBULL

from 'Transmutations'

THE WORST was that although the pain of their separation, like her love, had long ago receded, so that she could no longer even imagine what had kept them together and scarcely remembered the name of that other who had taken him from her,

the bitterness of her jealousy remained as suffocating as ever.

MARK OGLE

Setting a Candle

Only a steady hand can set a candle
To light a cold dark room,
With a deft twist of fingers,
Finding the still point swiftly and surely.

An unready hand trembles, falters,
Tries again, burns fingers
Coated with the tacky wax
And fails to find a steady light
Till peace and action melt
Into one flame, within my mind,
Before my eyes, the circling shadow
Wavering round the slender stem,
And the flame dips in salute to darkness,
And then swells suddenly to life again.

ACKNOWLEDGEMENTS

IAIN CRICHTON SMITH: 'New Year' from *A Country for Old Men* (Carcanet, 2000) by kind permission of the publisher;

TRACEY HERD: 'A Letter from Anna' from *Dead Redhead* (Bloodaxe, 2001) by kind permission of the author;

JAMES McGONIGAL: 'Turning Over in a Strange Bed' translated by Rody Gorman from *Across the Water – Irishness in Modern Scottish Literature* (Argyll Publishing, 2000) by kind permission of the author.

iynx publishing apologize for any errors or ommissions in the above list and would be grateful to be notified of any corrections that should be incorporated in the next edition or reprint of this volume.

A big thank you to: Ian McDonough, Brian Johnstone, Ken Cockburn, Stewart Conn, Roddy Lumsden, Donalda Smith, Deborah Nelken, Liz and Tom Short, and of course, Ali C.

Allan Crosbie was runner-up in the 1998 Arvon/Daily Telegraph poetry competition, and has had poetry published in many magazines and journals.
He was awarded a Scottish Arts Council Writer's Bursary in 1999.
He lives in Portobello with Alison and teaches English in Edinburgh.

Shore Poets: A Chronology

Shore Poets have organised monthly readings in a variety of Edinburgh venues since Autumn 1991. This chronology lists these venues, and the special events taking place over and above the monthly sessions.

1991
Founding of Shore Poets by Brian Johnstone and Ros Brackenbury.
First readings in October at the Shore Gallery, Leith.

1992
Events move in May to the 369 Gallery on the Cowgate.
Mark Ogle becomes the third organiser.
First anniversary reading features Norman MacCaig.
First group reading outwith Edinburgh, at Pittenweem Arts Festival.

1993
Another move, to the Tron Tavern at Hunter Square.
Ros Brackenbury leaves Scotland for the USA.
Shore Poets becomes a collective, and Stewart Conn becomes the group's president.
Group reading at Tulloch Castle, Dingwall.

1994
Publication and launch of the first Shore Poets anthology, *The Golden Goose Hour*, edited by Ros Brackenbury and Brian Johnstone.
Group readings at Clutha Vaults, Glasgow, and at Tulloch Castle.

1995
Group reading at the New Bazaar, Dumfries.
Poetry and Rebellion: Words and Music on a Jacobite Theme featuring Iain Crichton Smith takes place at the Café Royal.

1996
Shore Poets move to the Fruitmarket Gallery.
In May, Tom McGrath reads at the Filmhouse after a showing of *The Connection* as part of Shore Poets' contribution to the Centenary of Cinema celebrations.
Four lunchtime readings take place at Adam House as part of the Edinburgh Festival Fringe.
Fifth anniversary reading, *Take Five*, featured Gael Turnbull, Kathleen Jamie, Ros Brackenbury, and other members of Shore Poets reading work by their favourite dead poets. Incorporated a publication project written, printed and distributed on that day.
Publication and launch of the second Shore Poets anthology, *The Ice-Horses*, edited by Stewart Conn and Ian MacDonough.

1997
Reading at Glasgow Royal Concert Hall as part of the Celtic Connection Festival.
First Shore Poets reading at the Edinburgh Book Festival.

1998
A second event at the Edinburgh Book Festival, and one at the Kirkcudbright Arts Festival. In the Autumn the group moves to the cellar bar of the Canon's Gait.
A website is set up by Peter Cudmore.

1999
Death of Mark Ogle.

2000
Publication and launch of *A Memory of Fields* by Mark Ogle (Akros).
Allison Funk from Illinois reads in June.

2001
Tenth anniversary event at the Edinburgh International Book Festival.

LIST OF PUBLICATIONS

The Golden Goose Hour (Taranis Books, 1994), edited by Ros Brackenbury and Brian Johnstone;

Poetry and Rebellion: Words and Music on a Jacobite Theme, (Shore Poets, 1995), featuring 'The Ghost in the Snow' a specially commissioned poem by Iain Crichton Smith;

Birdcalls by Tom McGrath (Shore Poets, 1996);

Take Five, various authors, (Shore Poets, 1996);

The Ice-Horses (Scottish Cultural Press, 1996), edited by Stewart Conn and Ian MacDonough.